Water Your Garden

Caring for and Nurturing Your Wife

Gordon Skinner

Seldom Seen Press

© 2025 by Gordon Skinner

Published by Seldom Seen Press

PO Box 26632

Prescott Valley Arizona 86312

www.seldomseenpress.com

ISBN Paperback: 978-1-955759-35-9

ISBN eBook: 978-1-955759-44-1

To my Mom and my African sons

Contents

Preface

In writing this book, I set out to share some of the lessons I've learned over 30 years of marriage to my amazing wife, Teresa. My sincere hope is that "Water Your Garden" will enrich young marriages with practical, life-giving principles — and perhaps even breathe new life into relationships that have grown old or stale. If this book can help couples avoid the heartache of a withering marriage, it will have been worth writing. I pray that these pages bring renewed hope and fresh "water" to all your relationships.

Gordon Skinner

> Love, as noble as it is, cannot be called water until it is expressed by words and actions in a manner that your beloved can understand."

Introduction

I owe a big gratitude to my wife, who has encouraged me to write this short book because of the wonderful difference these principles have made in our marriage. Teresa and I both love the Lord and find joy in helping other people grow and succeed in their families and in their lives. It is our prayer that these Godly truths will serve to help you succeed in your marriage relationship and your friendships. I have found that many of these truths spill over into every relationship we have.

This book is written in simple, common language and the truths are deep and meaningful. They have changed my life and our marriage, and I would like to share them with you.

1
The Allegory

The other day I was invited by a friend to come to his house and look at his garden. He sounded desperate on the phone, so I agreed to look since he didn't live far away. As I pulled up, the front lawn was lush, freshly mowed, and he was blowing the clippings off the sidewalk. My friend offered me a few strawberries from a bowl on the front porch. When I commented on how tasty they were, he said the neighbor had given him some since his own garden was doing so poorly. He confessed that he had actually worked over there quite frequently as that garden was beautiful and fruitful.

We got right to the point, and he led me to his backyard where a pretty, white fence enclosed his vegetable garden. As I got closer, I could immediately see that there was a definite problem. Tomato vines were drooping, and the tips of the leaves were browning. In fact, the entire garden looked sad. Upon further inspection, I could see that the ground, which used to be soft and workable, had become hard and cracked. The few green beans on the vine were shriveled and dry. There was very little fruit anywhere. Even the usually beautiful roses along the fence were falling on the ground. Nothing was thriving except some weeds. In my friend's discouragement, he had given up pulling them out while they were small. The signs of neglect were evident everywhere. As I walked by the roses, I was viciously scratched by a few thorns.

This garden was in such poor condition I was tempted to tell my friend to give up hope. As I walked out the gate, something caught my attention. The supply line, which fed water to the whole garden, was pinched right where it went through the fence.

"Aha!" I exclaimed. "There's the problem. This garden has not been getting the regular water it needs."

Although this short allegory of my friend's garden never really happened, friends have often called me concerned and complaining about their marriage. Let's explore together how this story can help us understand our relationships with our wives.

Men are often aware that things are not going along smoothly, but they are at a loss to know what to do to fix it. Sadly, many marriages end up in divorce that could have been avoided. Much strife and heartbreak could have been resolved by a good, simple understanding of how to **Water Your Garden.**

Here are some of the comments I have heard from men who are struggle with understanding their wives:

- "Why is my wife acting so crazy?"
- "My wife and I just cannot get along."
- "Does this woman even love me?"
- "I totally do not understand this woman!"
- "I don't understand. What did I say wrong?"
- "Am I supposed to be a mind reader?"

Do these statements sound familiar?

2
Things are Looking Good on the Outside

My friend's lawn was very neat and well-kept where the neighbors could see, but the real problems were in the backyard, out of the view of their friends and neighbors.

To the public, a married couple might look perfectly manicured, happy, and beautiful. But, in the backyard, out of the public eye, there may be serious problems developing, which need urgent attention. Only a few close friends might hear the couple's concerns and their frustrated cries for help.

Publicly, a man may appear to be a great husband, but at home his wife does not feel the intimacy and care. She needs water in the "backyard" away from public view. When your wife feels like you have heard her from your heart, she will feel loved. She desires to share things, which are important to her with you, her friend. A man's attentiveness to what is happening in his wife's life and listening to the events of her day is often very meaningful.

NOTE:

Is your wife merely an afterthought, your servant, or is she honored by the way you treat her in front of other people?

Do you speak well of her to your friends?

While it is true that we need to nourish our wives in private, what is equally significant is how we honor her in public.

3
Signs of Neglect and Deterioration

My friend's garden showed clear signs of neglect — wilting tomato vines, dry and shriveled beans, and unkempt roses covered with thorns. This mirrors a marriage where, over time, neglect often leads to emotional withdrawal, frustration, and growing distance between partners. Just as the plants in the garden need attention and frequent care to thrive, a marriage requires consistent effort and nurturing. If a husband neglects to pay attention to his wife's emotional needs, their connection will weaken, and their relationship will deteriorate.

- **Marriage Parallel:** If a husband ignores the small things—like communication, affection, or support—his wife may feel emotionally starved, leading to frustration and hurt. The marriage will likely wilt if it's not properly cared for.

Let's be honest. Most men are quite self-centered and have lived their whole adult lives until they married doing what is best for themselves. Now that they are married, they have so much to learn and so many changes to make before the two become one.

Few of us enter marriage with an "A" in the class, which trained us to expertly identify the signs that our wife is lacking an essential ingredient to help her thrive. Perhaps you have not become aware of the warning signs that your marriage is not receiving enough care and attention. It is so helpful to carefully consider your wife and interpret the signs that her garden is not getting proper care. She will express it in many ways which might seem confusing at first.

Perhaps you can learn more quickly than I did to Water Your Garden. You will be happy you did!

4

Hardening of the Ground

The garden's soil had become hard and cracked, making it difficult for plants to take root or grow properly. Similarly, in a marriage, when a husband neglects to address emotional needs of his wife over time, this can cause emotional barrenness in the relationship. When a wife begins to harden her heart and allow bitterness to creep in, she can come to a place that even her husband's efforts to be kind may not sink in. Dry, hardened soil tends to let water run off.

- **Marriage Parallel:** When a husband neglects his wife for long periods, she may start to close herself off, becoming emotionally distant or withdrawn. Just as hard soil requires work and patience to soften, a marriage requires constant effort and emotional openness to ensure that the connection stays nurturing and fertile.

When I was younger, I needed to dig a short trench in the summer. Besides the heat, I found that the ground was incredibly hard and dry, almost like concrete. My father saw me picking away at the stubborn soil and stopped me for a minute to offer a suggestion. He said, "If you get the hose and run water slowly over the area you have to dig, it will make your job so much easier." Well, I was ready for a break anyway, so I dragged the hose over and began soaking the area. At first, the water puddled and ran off. It didn't seem that the ground could absorb anything. It was quite surprising to me. But, after a little while, the surface began to get wet, and the soil began to soak up the life giving liquid. What was once stubborn and resistant became receptive and pliable for me to work with.

When a marriage has been parched for too long, the hearts become resistant and even stubborn and untrusting of each other. When the original openness is lost, it might take some time of gentle, consistent watering before that life giving liquid takes effect, and the relationship flourishes again.

5
Weeds Taking Over

The weeds, which should have been plucked diligently when they were small, had been allowed to grow, unchecked and ignored. In marriage, neglecting small issues —unresolved conflicts, unaddressed feelings, or minor miscommunications—leads to the growth of weeds. Seemingly small issues, if left alone, can escalate into larger problems, overshadowing the positive aspects of the relationship.

- **Marriage Parallel**: Weeds can devour all the nutrients and water without producing any fruit. Weeds are comparable to minor issues and unresolved tensions that, when neglected, become very challenging to manage. Husbands must actively cultivate the marriage by addressing problems before they grow out of control, ensuring that love and peace thrive in the relationship.

What is consuming the nutrients and the water in your marriage? Are you so busy that there is no time or energy left for your spouse? How do you spend your leisure time? On yourself? Do you still have enough creative energy remaining after your job to conceive a plan for a special date night or fun activity together?

Understandably, men need a little alone time to relax after a demanding day's work, but now that you have your bride, you can learn new ways to relax, enjoy, and be refreshed. Also, consider that your dear wife might have had an equally challenging day. Do it together! Discover what helps you both relax and draws you closer together at the same time.

Spiritual Weeds

In a marriage, there are natural challenges that every human experiences. Beyond the experiences of being tired, offended, frustrated, or hurt, there is a spiritual war going on where the enemy has the intention to divide, deceive, and destroy all good things.

Your marriage is constantly under attack. When we realize that some of the greatest challenges in our marriages are inspired and magnified by demonic forces, we are already on the path to restore a thriving marriage. We know we have already been given the victory through our savior, Jesus Christ. But, unless we learn how to stand in the liberty we have been given, we will not be able to experience the joy God intended us to have. Be aware of the spiritual weeds that the enemy sows in our garden.

For example, have you ever unexpectedly felt like something was wrong? The entire way, driving home from work you felt disturbed. Perhaps, your mind was focused on harsh words, which had been spoken, or some other offense. When you arrived home, your wife also was in a sour mood and easily became upset. Suddenly, for no apparent reason, you both were at odds. Well, the enemy had been busy whispering in your ear and in her mind as well. If these kinds of thoughts and lies are not dealt with intentionally, they grow up and choke the love and steal the sweet fellowship. Left alone, these devilish influences cause you to distrust and dislike one another and even completely divide your relationship.

> So then, surrender to God. Stand up to the devil and resist him and he will turn and run from you. 8 Move your heart closer and closer to God, and He will come even closer to you. But make sure you cleanse your life, you sinners, and keep your heart pure and stop doubting.
>
> — James 4:7-8 TPT

James identifies these weeds and shows us how to live weed free:

1. Pull the weeds of self-will and selfish living. Stop doing your own thing and daily surrender your plans to the Lord. Daily seek His will and His attitudes. Desire to live the Beatitudes.
2. Actively and intentionally identify and resist the devil's lies and purposely choose the truth.
3. Daily draw your heart close to God. Connect with Him continually during the day.
4. Cleanse your life from sinful habits and activities that open doors for your flesh and the devil to work.
5. Keep your heart pure. Jesus said, "Blessed are the pure in heart for they will see God." A pure heart will lead to a fruitful life. Repent often and remain humble.
6. Stop doubts and fill your heart and life with faith and truth. Identifying doubts are not so difficult because the symptoms of anxiousness, worry, regrets, and fears all lead to a diagnosis of a condition called doubt, which means a lack of trust in a loving all powerful God.

A Powerful Tool for Pulling Weeds

There are seven words, which spoken often, at the appropriate time, are a tool, which will keep weeds from growing larger. "What is this amazing tool called?" you might ask. I will give you the secret. However, this tool is not easy for a proud man to use. Only the humble may find its use effective. Self-centered men cannot perceive its necessity, and many have lost it among the weeds. But, for those who have become adept at this tool's function, it is a treasure. Here are the words. I will reveal their wonder working secret:

"Forgive me. I was wrong. I'm sorry."

6
The Thorny Roses

The roses, which should have been beautiful and uplifting, have become a source of pain. Their sharp thorns scratch at the husband. In a similar way, when a husband neglects to nurture the emotional and relational aspects of the marriage, even things that were once beautiful—like shared moments, affection, and connection—can become painful or alienating.

- **Marriage Parallel:** When a husband fails to nurture his wife or is emotionally absent, she may feel hurt or emotionally bruised by his lack of attention. A loving, beautiful wife, out of her frustration and need might become thorny and hurtful as she seeks to get his attention or to act out her troubled emotions.

Thorns or Roses, often it's your choice

When is the last time you told your wife, "I love you" or "I think you are beautiful"? Have you told your spouse lately that you think they are gifted and amazing? The more roses are appreciated, the more they bloom.

I have taken up the habit of telling my wife how amazing she is. Although this is very true, she needs to hear it from me. This simple practice provides validation and encouragement to her. Simply saying the words, "You are amazing!" is water to her soul.

When you, her king, tell your bride that she is beautiful, you will see her bloom more gorgeously. Every wife has a short memory in this area and needs to be told how much you love her several times a day. She already knows you love her factually, but she needs to hear it often to feel it in her heart.

Go ahead, guys, you can make your roses bloom!

Give them the right nutrients and a little faithful watering. Learn to water with a compliment.

7
The Pinched Water Supply

The key problem in the garden, as revealed in the short story, is that the water supply has been pinched, preventing the plants from getting the hydration they need to grow. This represents one of the most crucial aspects of the garden—without water, no plant can thrive. Similarly, in a marriage, emotional connection and support are like the water that nourishes your wife. Without regular emotional support, validation, and nurturing, your wife cannot flourish.

- **Marriage Parallel**: Dear husband, you may be unintentionally pinching the flow of emotional care by neglecting your wife's needs for affection, communication, time, and intimacy. By not ensuring a steady flow of emotional support, your marriage risks becoming dry and barren. Many ill effects come from this single problem.

What Does Water Represent?

In this allegory about marriage, water speaks of giving our garden attention, thoughtful care, physical touch, intimacy, and transparent conversations—just to mention a few examples.

For love to be understood, it must be expressed in the language that your wife understands. Have you noticed what moves your wife the most? What do you say or do that means "I love you" to her? Is it a special date night, just you and her? Perhaps a compliment about something she has done? A thoughtful little gift maybe? A simple hug or tender touch? Calling her occasionally when you are out to see how she is doing? Perhaps selflessly doing something about that squeaky front door or sagging ceiling? Would sharing something special that happened in your day make her feel that she is your special friend? For some couples, serving others together or doing a special joint project will communicate that "we are one".

> "Love, as noble as it is, cannot be called 'water' until it is expressed by words and actions in a manner that your beloved can understand."

Every plant in the garden needs water. Each variety requires a little different nurturing to thrive. No garden can thrive without that essential need for water being provided. Tomatoes need support so they don't get dragged down by their fruit. Potatoes do better if they are hilled up with dirt to prevent the sun from turning their fruit green (and toxic). Carrots prefer soft and sandy soil. Some plants do better in shade while others love the full heat of the afternoon sun. Each plant needs your care and love **in a different way.**

The love we give is the water, which causes our dear wife, i.e., our garden, to flourish.

- A good gardener is willing to study what his garden needs differently in every section.
- A good gardener gives his garden daily attention.
- A good gardener quickly notices when a few leaves begin to wither and turn brown.
- A good gardener is diligent to pull out weeds (deal with problems) while they are small.
- Divorce is never an option.
- Water frequently.
- Pull weeds early.
- Prune wisely and gently.
- Give your time.
- Seek to understand.

8
Recognition and a Solution

At the end of the allegory, we see the real issue—the blocked water supply—the real reason the garden is failing. Husbands, we must recognize that unless we change our behavior, we cannot restore health and vitality to our marriage. The solution isn't to abandon the garden, but to provide the proper care and nourishment it needs. Men, are you willing to go on this journey with me to learn what it means to Water Your Garden?

- **Marriage Parallel:** Just as the friend must address the root problem (lack of water) to restore the garden, a husband must identify and address the core issues in the marriage—lack of communication, emotional neglect, or insufficient affection. Recognizing our need to learn how to consistently nurture our wives, both physically and emotionally, is the first step to fixing the relationship.

The easiest problems to see are always in someone else's life. The hardest ones are in our own. In the same way, we have the hardest time realizing that we might have weaknesses and learning gaps. No one is born with all the skills needed to succeed at life, especially at something as complicated as marriage and family. Again, the first step toward resolving the issues in our own garden is to recognize that there is a problem and to believe that there are solutions that lead to a peaceful, fulfilling marriage with consistent effort.

Can you believe that things can be beautiful in your home? Remember the verse: Now, Faith is the substance of things hoped for, the evidence (persuasion) of things not (yet) seen. Can you base your hope on something you have not yet experienced in your marriage? Maybe you have seen other marriages that appear to be so wonderful, but you have no vision (faith) for how yours can also be wonderfully blessed. Many men give up hope because they only can see things the way they are through their physical eyes without trusting God to help, guide, and bless. Can you patiently trust God while He is changing you and believe He is working on your spouse as well?

Sharing your vision together with your wife can help you through the rough times.

**"I believe in us, and
I trust God to mold us together."**

9

Restoration Through Care

The allegory ends on a hopeful note as we identified the cause of the problem (the pinched water line). What is implied is that, with the right attention, the garden can recover. There is hope that you will see the garden thrive again. In marriage, once a husband recognizes the neglect and addresses the underlying causes, the relationship can be restored. Like tending to a garden, marriage requires ongoing effort—watering, weeding, and pruning to ensure that it remains healthy and vibrant and produces delightful fruit.

- **Marriage Parallel:** A marriage, like a garden, can also be restored through consistent effort. When the husband becomes aware of his wife's needs and makes a conscious effort to care for her emotionally, the relationship can grow and flourish once again. This restoration requires time, patience, and a willingness to put in the work to nurture the relationship.

The Bible teaches us that a husband should give his wife what she needs to grow and mature helping her to thrive and to flourish. This is what it means to nurture. Just as each variety of plant is different, women all have their own emotional, mental, spiritual, and physical needs. When she is loved in a way that meets these needs, she can be fruitful and more loving as a wife. In fact, this is what it means to cherish.

> So ought men to **love their wives as their own bodies**. He that loveth his wife loveth himself. **29** No man ever yet hated his own flesh; but **nourisheth** and **cherisheth** it, even as the Lord the church: **33** Nevertheless let every one of you in particular so **love his wife even as himself**; and the wife *see* that she reverence *her* husband.
>
> — Ephesians 5:28-29, 33 KJV

Here are the Greek definitions of these words:

Nourish - *ektrephō*

Thayer Definition:

1. to nourish up to maturity, to nourish
2. to nurture, bring up

Mounce adds: promote health and strength

Cherish - *thalpō*

Thayer Definition:

- to warm, keep warm
- to cherish with tender love, to foster with tender care

10
The Neighbor's Fruit

My friend offered me some very tasty fruit, which did not come from spending time in his own garden. He had been helping his neighbor. This implies that he had been distracted from his own garden and was investing his time and attention elsewhere—and getting some nice fruit as well.

- **Marriage Parallel:** When men become discouraged and frustrated at home, they will often find other interests to fill their own needs. He might be more respected and appreciated next door or at the office, club, team, etc. There is no replacement for your quality time and attention at home when it comes to strengthening a relationship. When you are absent or distracted, this is noticed and interpreted as, "I don't feel like he loves me as much as...." A wife becomes more vulnerable to a

kind gentleman pouring water on her parched
soul.

> Drink water from your own cistern and running
> water from your own well. 16 Should your
> springs be dispersed outside, your streams of
> water in the wide plazas? 17 Let them be for
> yourself alone, and not for strangers with you.
> 18 May your fountain be blessed, and may you
> **rejoice in the wife you married** in your youth
> –

— Proverbs 5:15-18 NET

> 12 Dear lover and friend, you're a secret garden, a
> private and pure fountain. 15 A garden
> fountain, sparkling and splashing, fed by
> spring waters from the Lebanon mountains.

— Song of Solomon 4:12,15 MSG

11

We Were Created Different

Let's summarize. In both the allegory and marriage, neglect leads to deterioration, but recognition of the core issues, such as a lack of emotional support, communication, or care, opens the path to recovery. Just as a garden needs regular care to thrive, a marriage requires consistent nurturing, attention, and love. The husband, like the gardener, must learn to provide the water of emotional support, address issues before they become weeds, and tend to his wife with the same care and commitment that one would show to a precious garden.

Mom's Advice:

> One of the most helpful things a husband can do for his wife is to be attentive to her needs. A woman's mind is like spaghetti, and

a man's like a waffle. A woman's mind is all inter-connected. There are emotions, facts, relationships, memories, fears and hopes and the consideration of other people's reactions all interacting at the same time. She can multitask well where the man can focus everything on a single project or develop a detailed plan. When the two learn to blend their strengths, they can both plan and consider all the people who might be affected.

— Karol Skinner (Mom)

...a man's mind is like a waffle.

In reality, it is common for a man to be doing nothing in his mind where a woman's mind is seldom idle.

Husbands, it's important to recognize that the way men and women think can be very different, and this is reflected in Scripture. For instance, Proverbs 31 describes a woman who is constantly attentive to her household, considering the needs of others and planning for the future (Proverbs 31:15-18). You can see how deeply engaged her mind is in various tasks and how she works to care for others. Meanwhile, men may experience times of stillness in their minds when they are not actively thinking about anything. This is not wrong, but understanding this difference can help you appreciate your wife's constant mental activity.

Ephesians 5:25 calls husbands to love their wives as Christ loves the church—sacrificially and attentively. This means being patient and understanding even when your wife's mind seems overly occupied and offering support in a way that acknowledges the mental load she often carries. By listening, encouraging, and showing empathy, you reflect the love and care that Scripture calls you to, fostering a deeper, more harmonious relationship.

Now that we understand our differences, we can begin to discover how to compliment each other?

12
Helpful Advice

Men often think that they must have an answer for all the millions of things his wife is concerned about. No! She needs to feel that you are hearing her and caring about what she is saying. How can you help your spouse to feel heard? It is called active listening. Do not try to solve her problem!

Explanation of Active Listening

Active listening involves fully focusing on your wife, understanding her message, and responding thoughtfully. A husband can practice this by:

- Giving undivided attention: Put away distractions (phone, TV) and maintain eye contact.
- Showing empathy: Acknowledge her feelings, even if you don't fully agree.

- Paraphrasing: Repeat back what she says in your own words to confirm understanding.
- Asking open-ended questions: Encourage her to share more by asking questions like, "How did that make you feel?" or "what happened then?"
- Avoiding interruptions: Let her finish speaking without offering your response or advice.
- Offering validation: Express understanding and support.

This approach fosters better communication and strengthens the emotional connection. Practice listening without offering advice unless your wife asks for it. Most of the time you can minister to her more by helping her feel heard than by you solving her issues. Later, if you believe you have a solid solution to an issue you can say, "I've been thinking about what you were saying, and I would like to offer an idea."

Here is a verse that has helped me realize that God will supply what I need to be a spring of water to my wife:

> The LORD will continually lead you; he will feed you even in parched regions. He will give you renewed strength, and you will be like a well-watered garden, like a spring that continually produces water.
>
> — Isaiah 58:11 NET

Men often feel overwhelmed by how many concerns their wife has. Remember, He will strengthen you and fill you with an endless supply of God's wisdom and grace to draw on if you will learn how to access it.

Here are three areas that might help you avoid becoming stressed when your wife's emotions become stirred about a problem that she is expressing to you.

1. Learn how powerful active listening is and become great at it.
2. Learn to develop a habit of spontaneously praying together about the concerns she expresses.
3. Learn to draw on God's wisdom and grace for these situations. It is your priestly position in the home to be used by God to speak His understanding and wisdom into family situations.

We will have to learn to:

"Lean not on your own understanding... In all your ways acknowledge Him and trust in His direction."

— See Proverbs 3:5

13
Bonus Chapter

The last chapter of Proverbs, chapter 31, gives a description of a woman of virtue. You likely have heard about her excellent qualities, but have you wondered what kind of husband she had? What a wonderful woman she is, "more valuable than rubies." We also read that her husband, who is known at the gates, can **trust her.** (To "sit at the gates" means the husband was a leader in his community since the judges and leaders would meet there). If this man did not **support, encourage, and empower** his wife, she could not have been so industrious. Many cultures suppress women and treat them as far less than their husbands—simply as property. This approach seriously hinders their wives.

> Husbands, in the same way, treat your wives with
> consideration as the weaker partners and
> show them **honor** as fellow heirs of the grace

of life. In this way <u>nothing will hinder your prayers.</u>

— 1 Peter 3:7 NET

Husbands, God's order is that you are the head even as Christ is the head of the church, but don't miss the rest of that verse, which says, "and gave himself for her." Jesus, our groom has given His life for us and has promised to go prepare a place for us. As you lead your family, consider their needs and weaknesses. Take responsibility by faith to provide what they need emotionally, physically, and spiritually. God will help you, give you wisdom and strength to fill your position in your marriage with the wife God gave as your helpmate.

Men, please realize that your wife is also learning, so be patient and understanding. The effect of culture has made marriage difficult as women are encouraged to assert their rights and men are led to abandon their responsibility. The enemy has targeted this holy union. Remember, the family your wife came from has a strong influence on her understanding of your individual roles. If you have an opportunity to shadow a godly couple with a happy marriage, you both will gain better perspective.

Men, God's word says you are the leader in the home, but what sort of leader are you? Do you tend to be quite militant and expect your wife to march to your orders or are you so soft that you do not lead at all. Both extremes will likely frustrate your wife. You and your spouse are a team, she will thrive if you two become one team. You can only learn true Godly leadership from the Word of God, fellowship with God and God's people. It is wisdom to connect yourself with a group of men who love God and are transparent with one another.

I have seen other husbands in the Bible who gave their wives the honor and freedom they needed to thrive. If Joseph had put away Mary or had her stoned as their law allowed, would we have Jesus the Savior today? How about Boaz? If he had let Ruth and Naomi starve, we would not have had King David. Instead, he protected her, helped her to glean in the best areas, and finally took his place as a kinsman redeemer. You can read this story in the book of Ruth.

A Helpful Truth

When God created Adam and Eve, the scripture tells us that He created **them** in His image.

> God created humankind in his own image, **in the image of God he created them,** male and female he created **them**.
>
> — Genesis 1:27 NET

When I came to understand that he created male and female different in many ways, I began to appreciate the differences. He gifted some of His nature and abilities to men who tend to be the protector, the provider, and the builder. However, one of the names of God is, "The

Breasted One" (El Shaddai), which reveals his caring, nurturing, and fostering attributes. These abilities are much more evident in women. Now, our God is neither male nor female, but He created humans in this way, giving special features and abilities to each one. When the two become one, we can realize more fully the image of God.

He is the Lion and the Lamb, the Judge and the Sacrifice, our Peace and the God of Justice. We see in Scripture that He reveals both His wrath and His grace, His truth and His mercy, His kindness and His severity. He is all of that! Perfect order and complete freedom. We can only strive to learn to live this way. We can see the best example in Jesus' life as he demonstrated His Father's nature.

> "As we walk with God and grow to be spiritual men who can live out our spiritual maturity in a natural way at home, we become a well-watered garden ourselves and a spring of water to our wives."
>
> — See Isaiah 58:10-11

14
Invitation

I invite you to welcome Jesus into your life and into your marriage. He is The Water of Life. He is Love. We cannot love unconditionally like God loves unless we choose to welcome Him into every part of our lives.

Here is a prayer of surrender to Him: Lord Jesus, I believe you are God's Son, and I choose to surrender my life to you. Please come into my life and into our marriage. Please forgive me for living to please myself and help me to love my wife with the love which you give. I confess that I have allowed my garden to suffer from a lack of water. I realize now that it is my responsibility to nurture and cherish my wife, and I know that I need your help. I choose now to make every effort to lead my family with the wisdom that you will give me. Help me now I pray. In Jesus name, Amen!

About the Author

Gordon Skinner, originally from Canada, has devoted his life to humanitarian service since 1985. After beginning his career in automotive technology, he felt a call to serve and shifted his focus to feeding the hungry, disaster relief, and international missions. His work has taken him to over a dozen countries, where he has taught agriculture, water purification, community development, and relationship-building skills. He co-founded the Antelope Valley Disaster Relief Network and served as Chairman of its Executive Board. Now based in Arizona, Gordon continues his mission as a chaplain and ordained minister with All Nations International, mentoring leaders both locally and around the world.

www.ingramcontent.com/pod-product-compliance
Lightning Source LLC
Chambersburg PA
CBHW070031030426

42335CB00017B/2384